It's been more than 10 years now.

I've come to believe that each shot is a fleeting effort to capture what cannot be captured—people with cameras grasping at the brim of life. I find this effort to be both beautifully unproductive and touching. We could never reproduce the full depth of an experience, and yet, we still take out our devices to try and preserve the parts we can. For me, photography is an ongoing struggle to find worth within a second when years exist; worth within a minute where centuries prevail.

Nature—I describe as an alluring, persistent, and incomprehensible force. You, me, and the creations that baffle us. That lizard chillin' on a leaf, the marks sketched into your subway seat, flowers in telephone poles, that random person smiling cheek to cheek grabbing hot cheetos at walmart... It's the most fascinating story in the world.

Whether the fly deserved to be eaten by the frog is beyond me, but I've been given the opportunity to perceive and capture the light bouncing off of it. Further, by learning the craft of those before me, I can manipulate this light to communicate a story within myself. Burdened with appreciation, empowered by intention, I can be beautifully unproductive. In sharing our story, each second has agency because the fleeting moments are full. There is no mundane, simply because I've found too much evidence against it.

There is life behind this light.

2020

nope

colorized ÷ 28mm ÷ f/5.6 ÷ 1/60

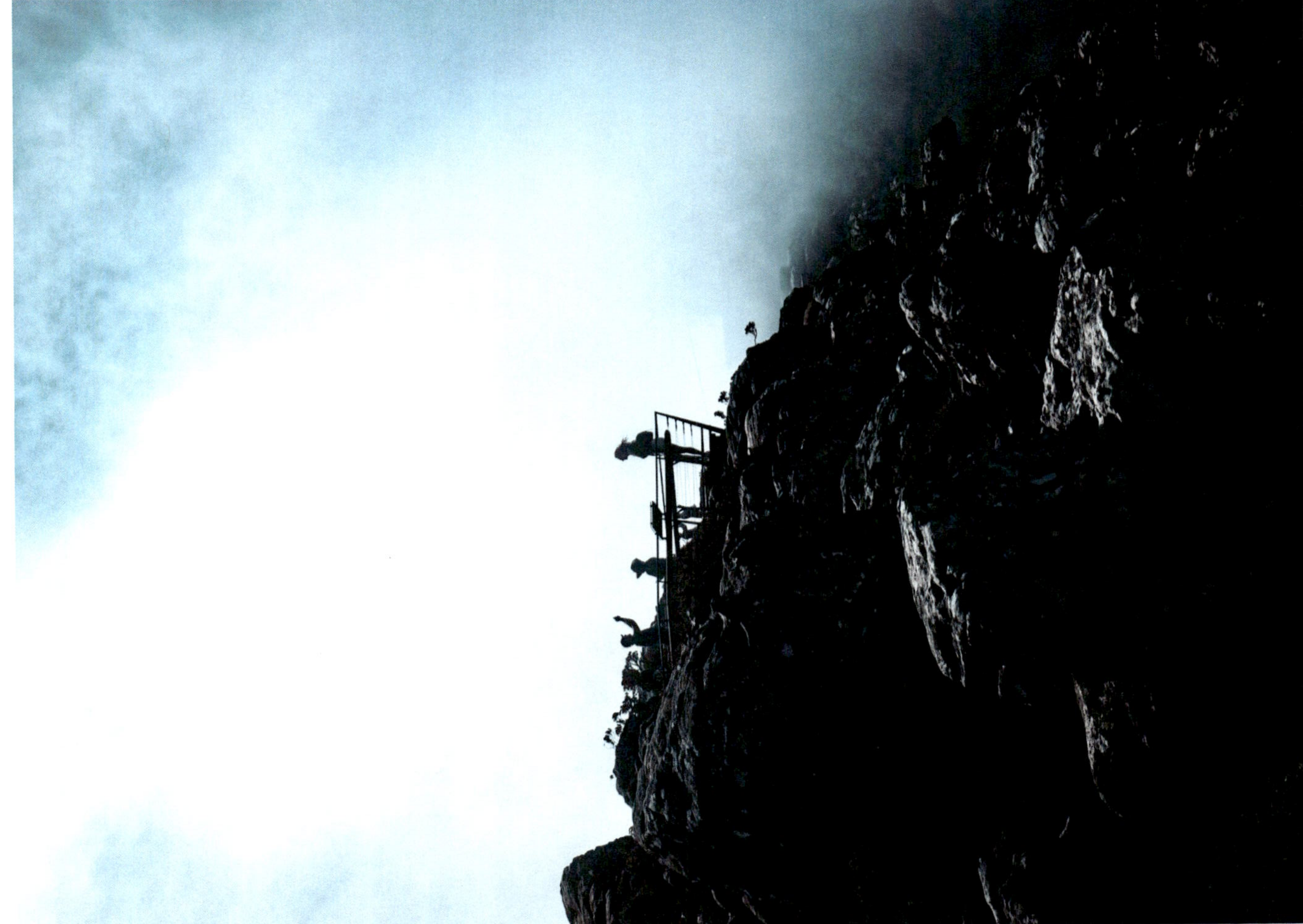

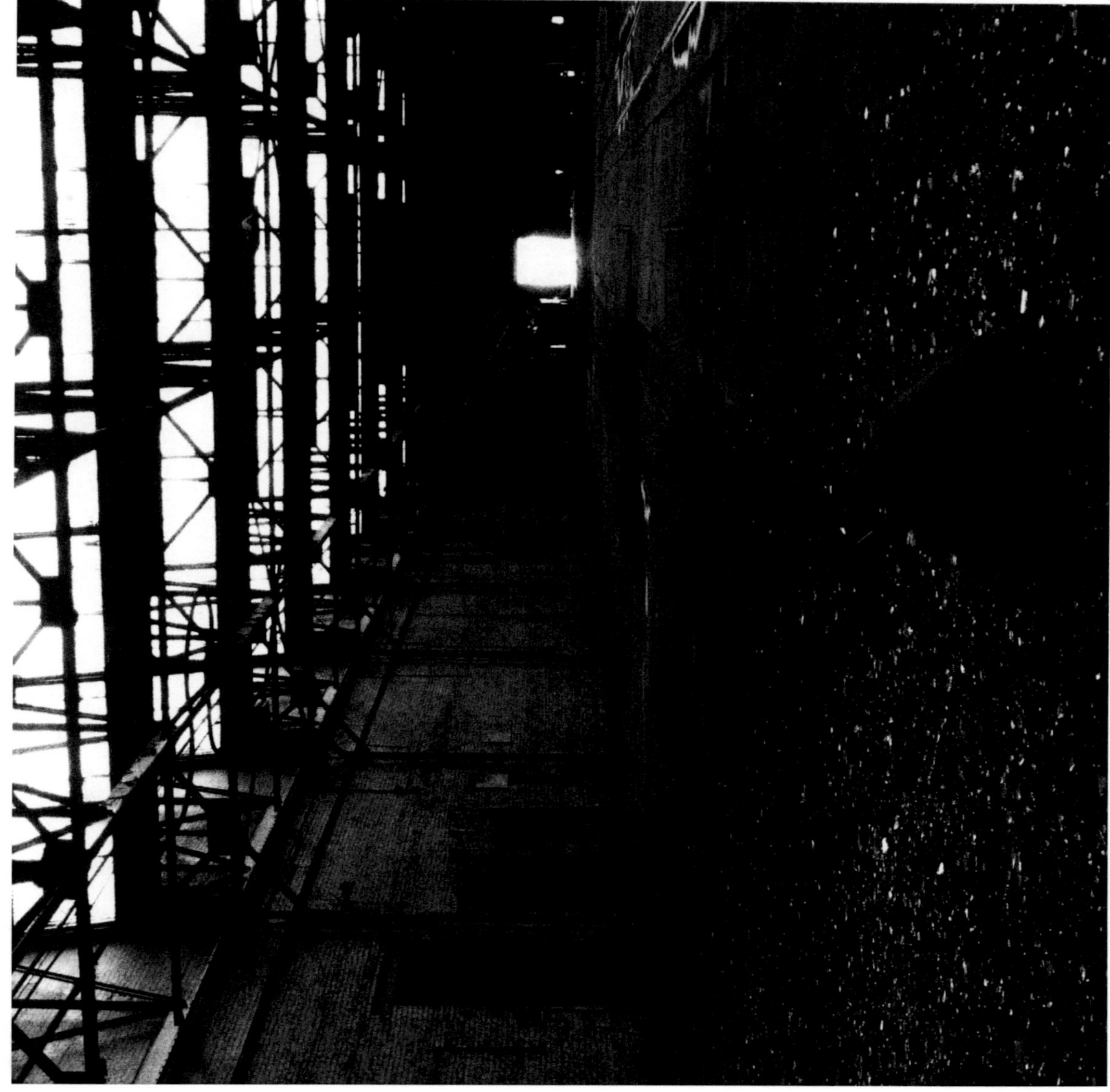
RIF   24mm ÷ f/11 ÷ 1/100   2018

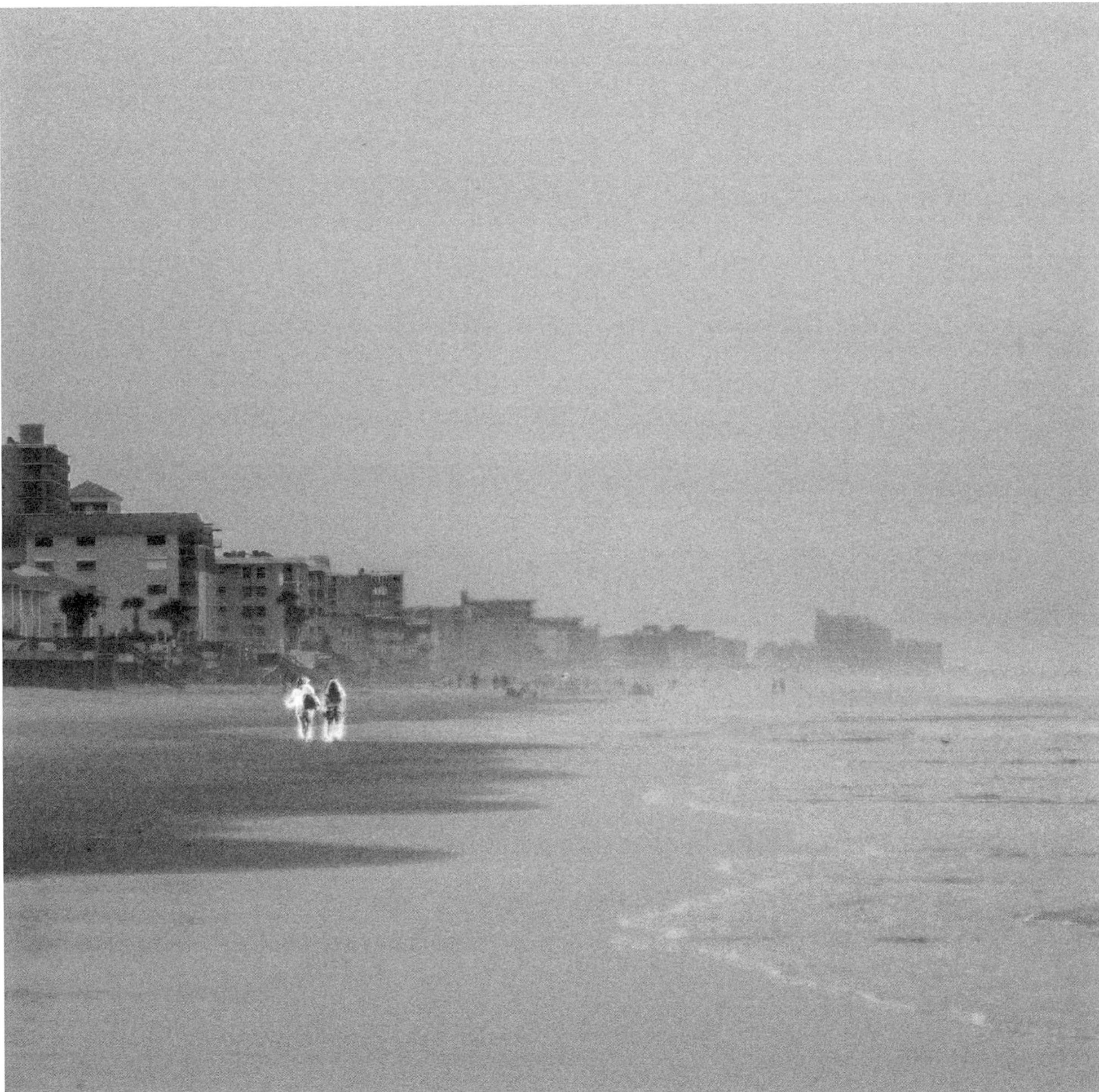

to here knows when
selective burn ✧ 105mm ✧ f/4 ✧ 1/200
2022

moth approved

75mm ✧ f/22 ✧ 2s

2015

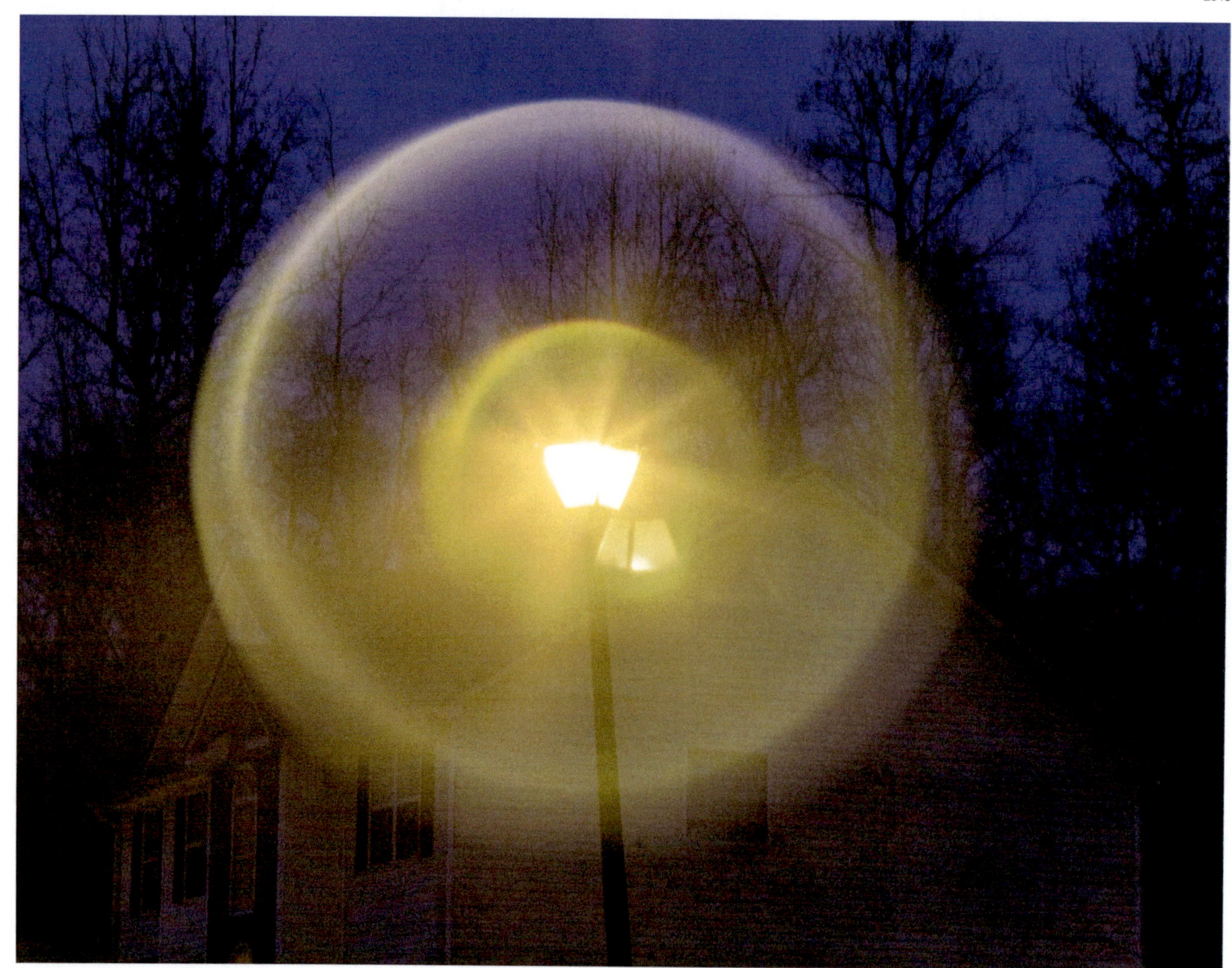

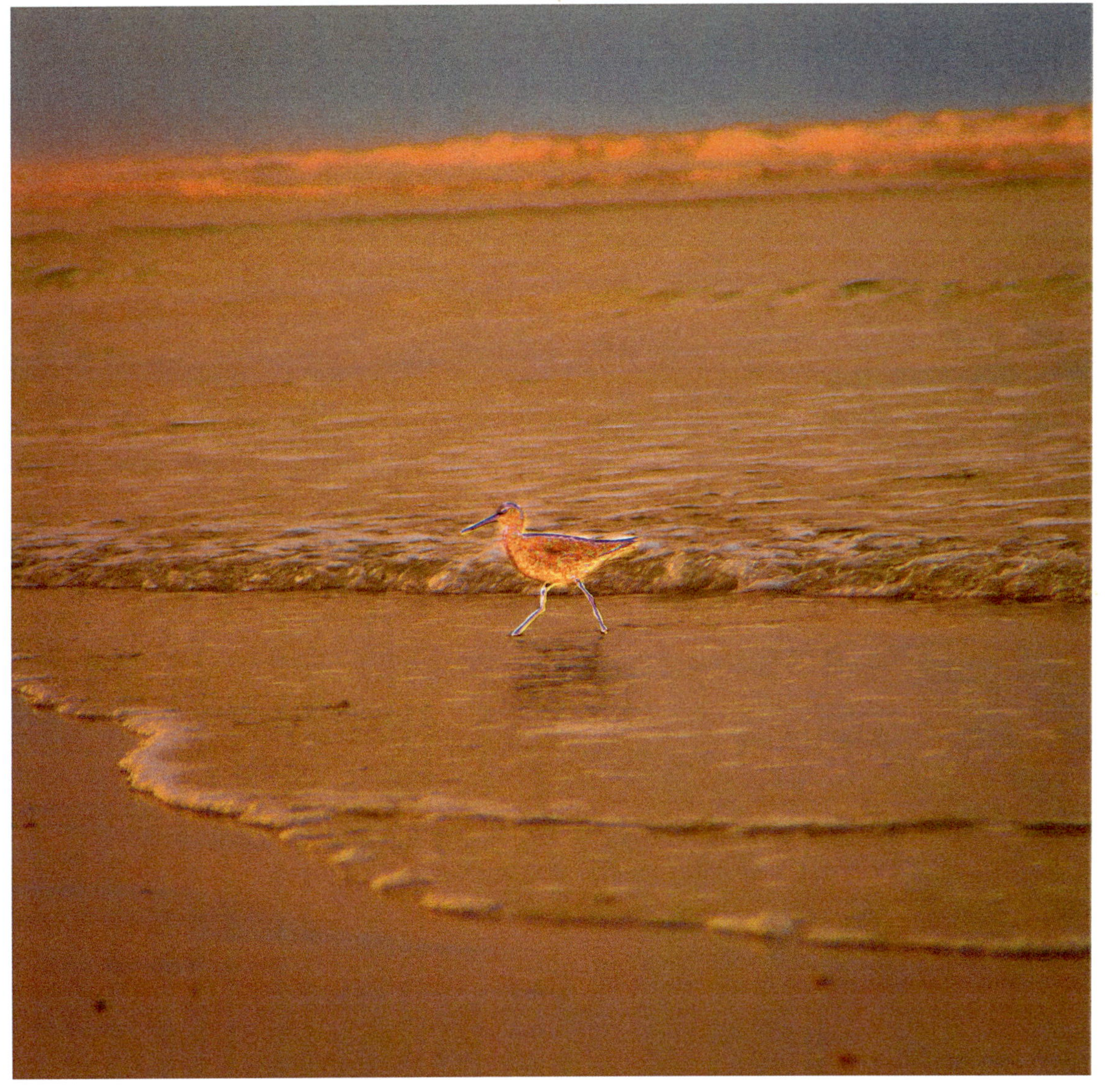

runts   flash ⬦ selective burn ⬦ 105mm ⬦ f/4 ⬦ 1/200   2017

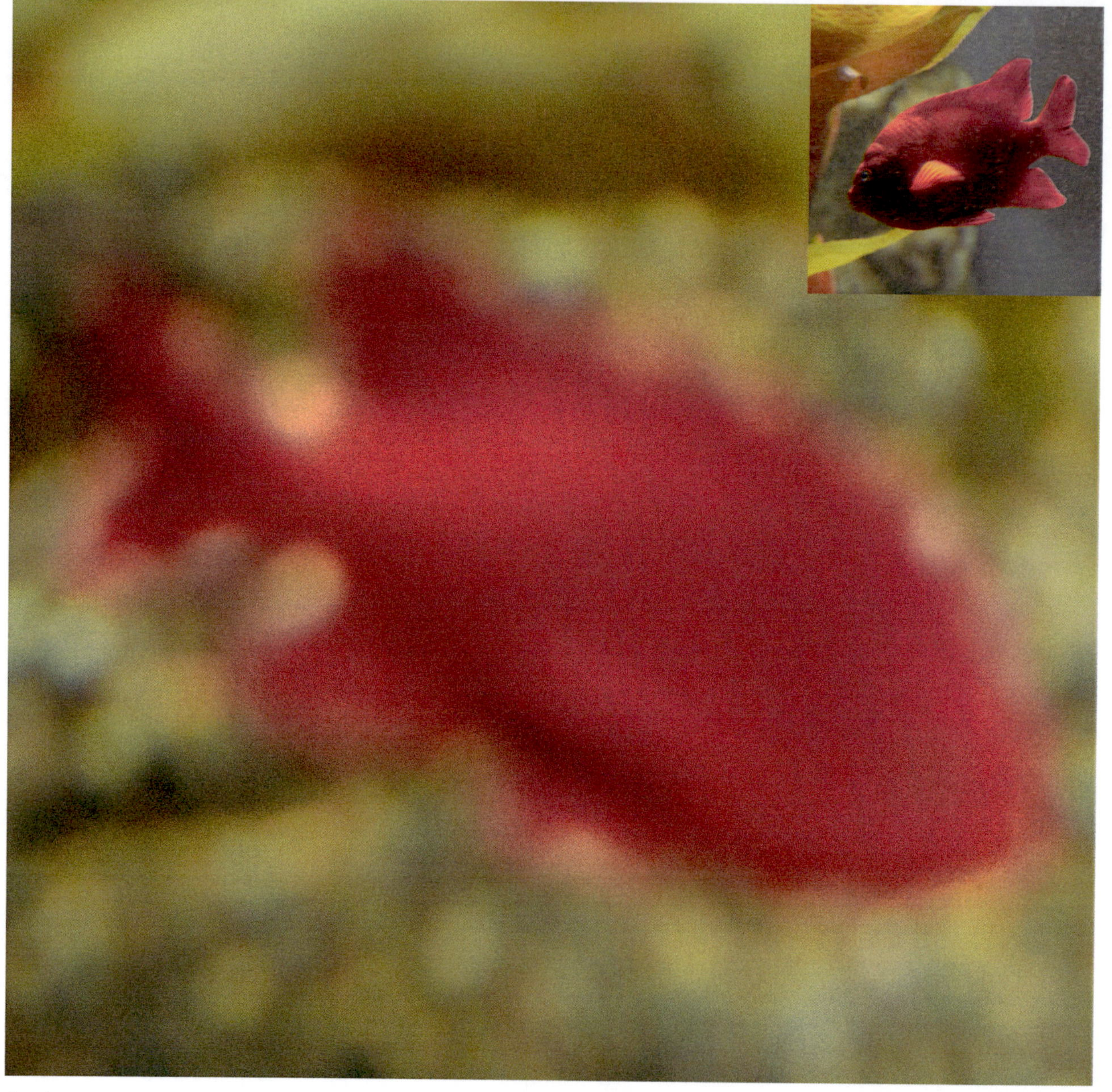

pitu cachaça
73mm & 92mm ÷ f/4 ÷ 1/100
2023

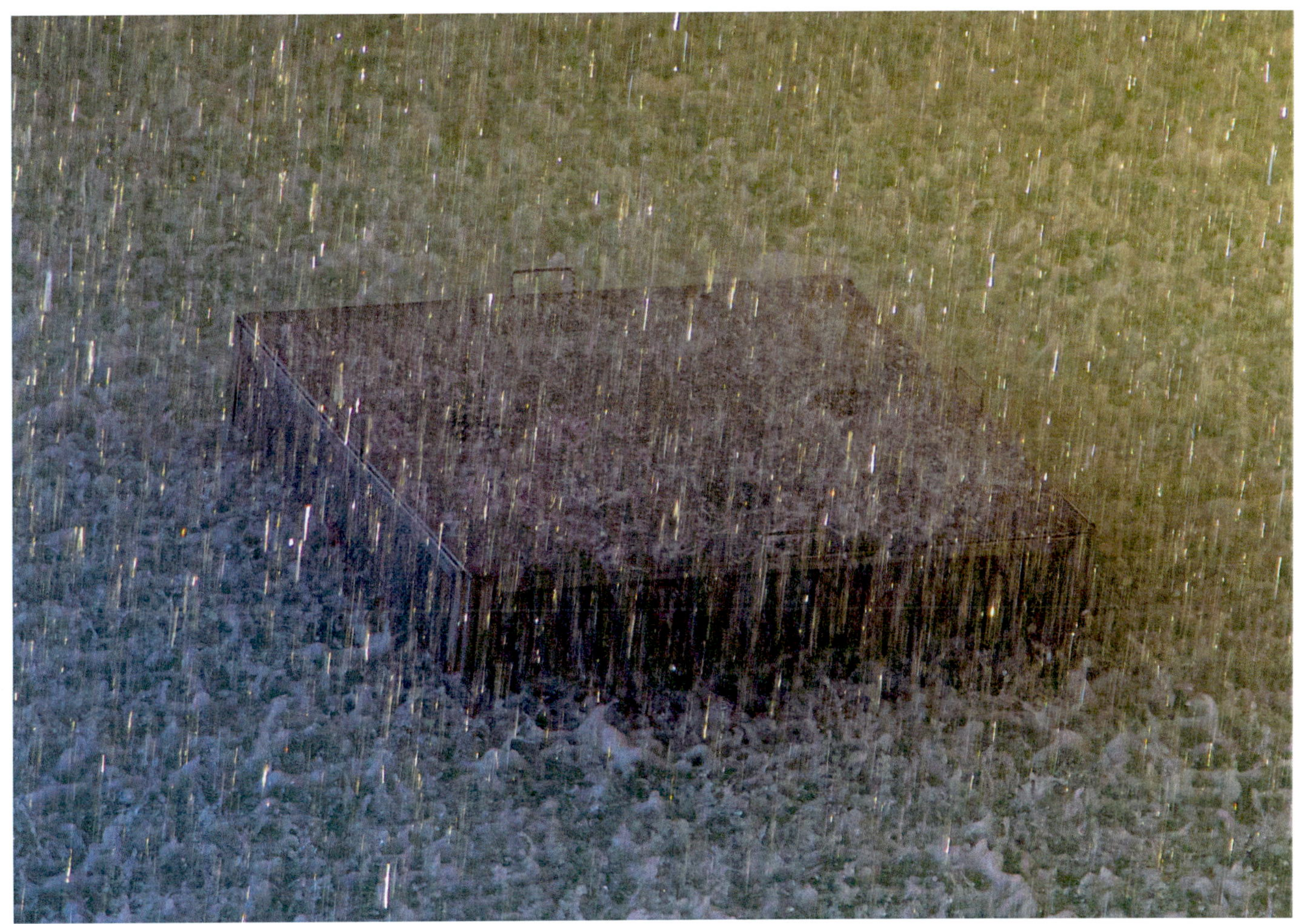

ybor 2am
105mm ÷ f/5.6 ÷ 1/100
2016

colorized ✦ 105mm ✦ f/11 ✦ 1/80

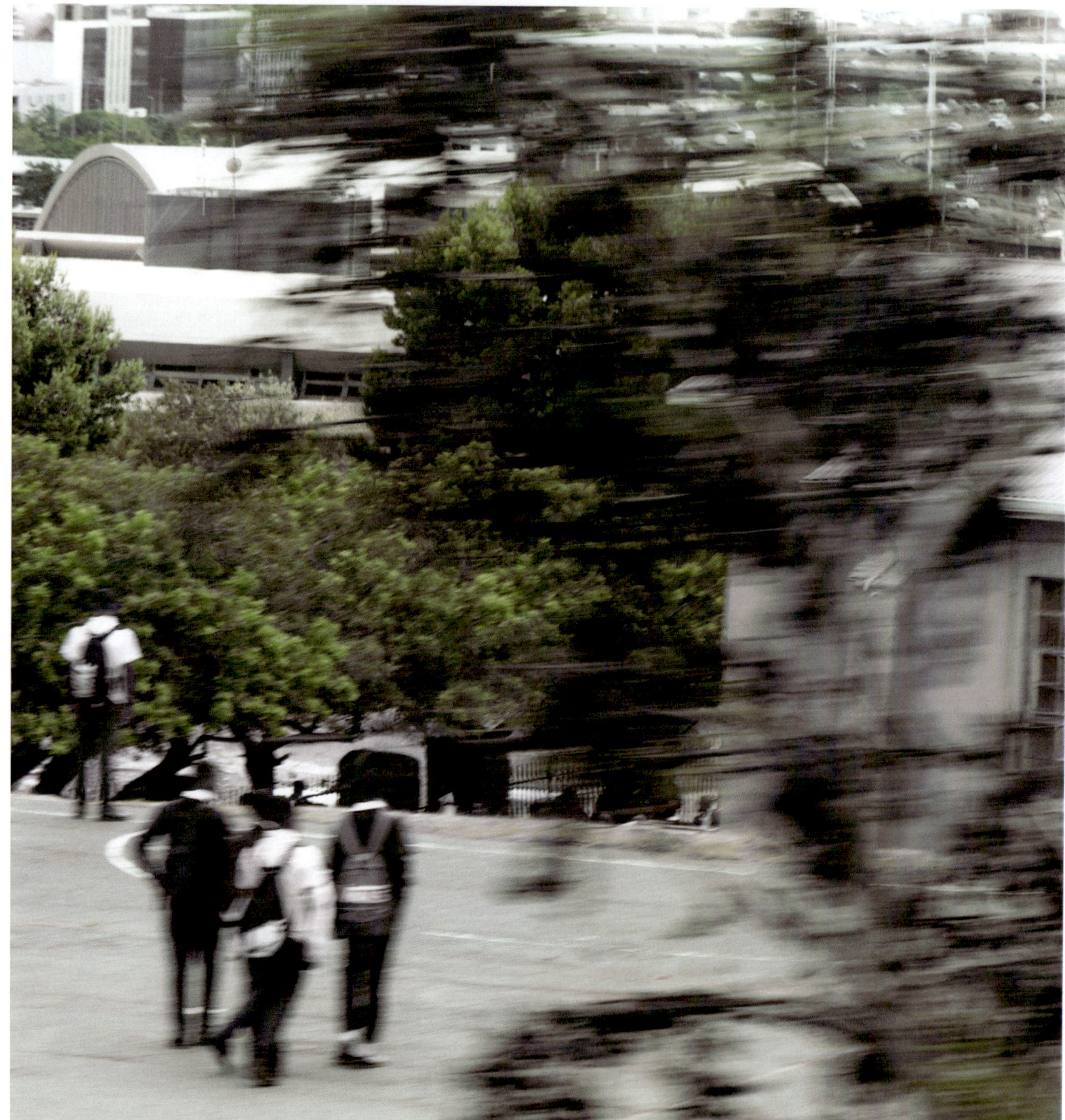

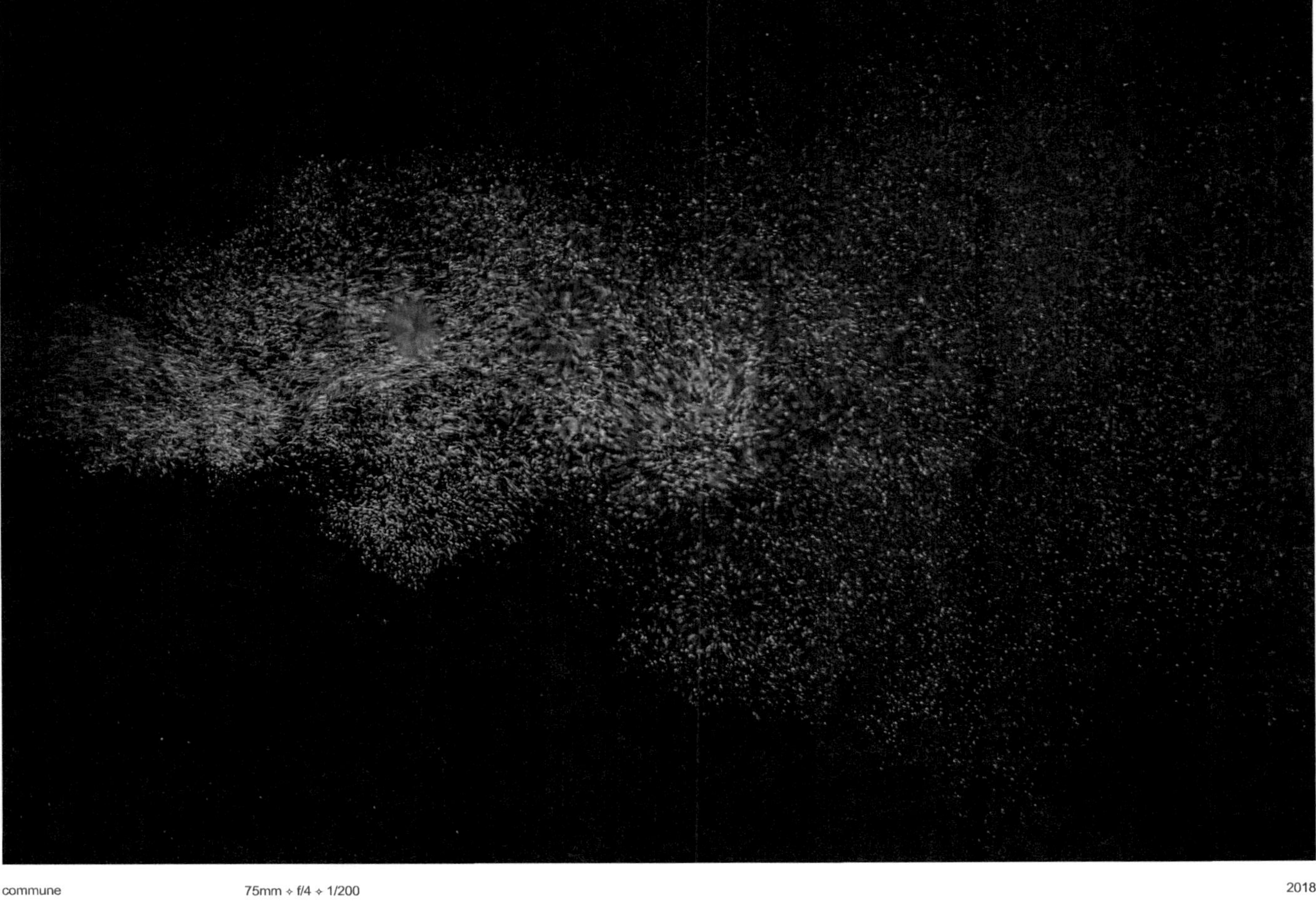
commune
75mm ✧ f/4 ✧ 1/200
2018

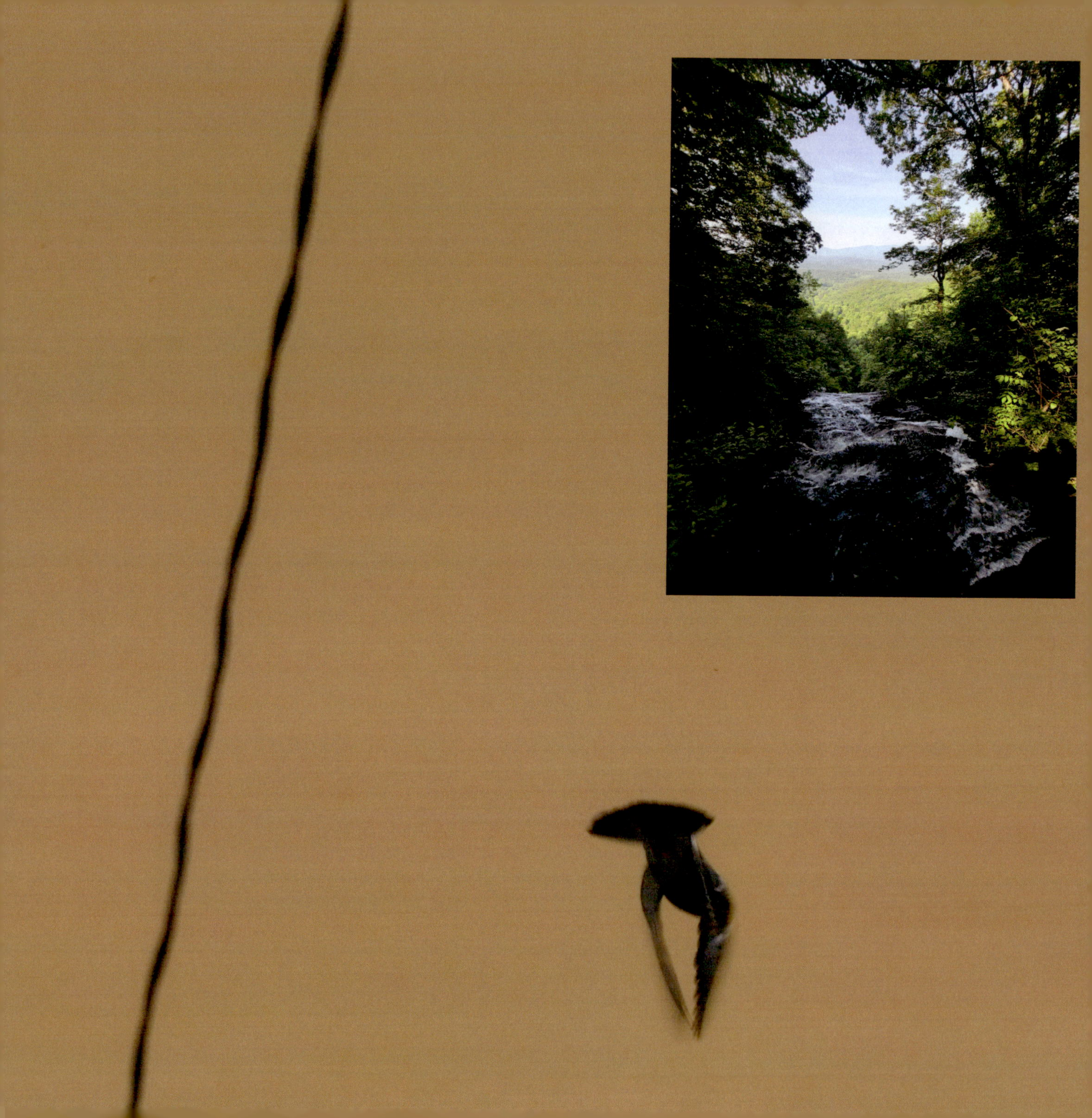

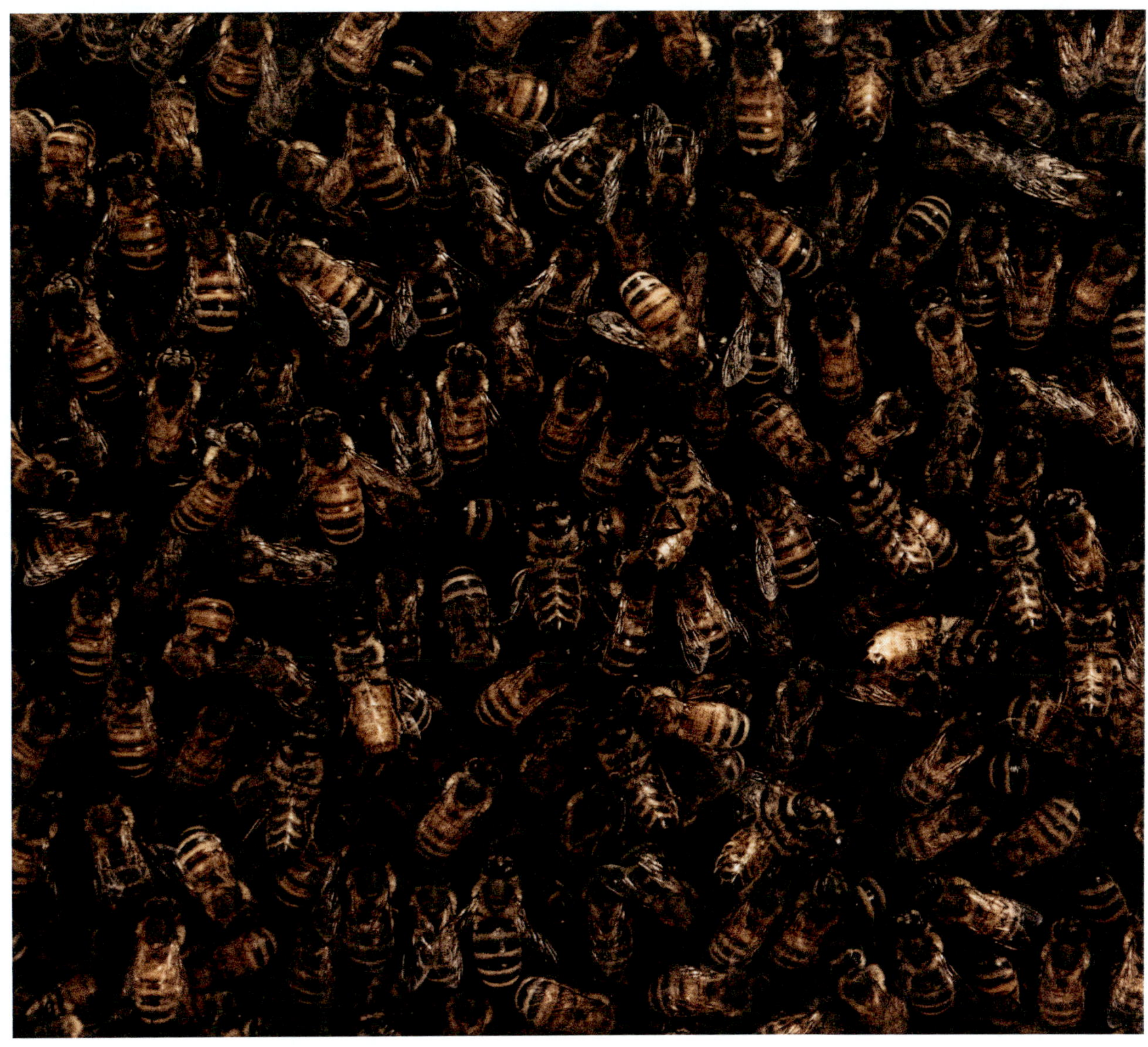

2017

simps

55mm ÷ f/5.6 ÷ 1/100

24mm ✧ f/11 ✧ 1/200

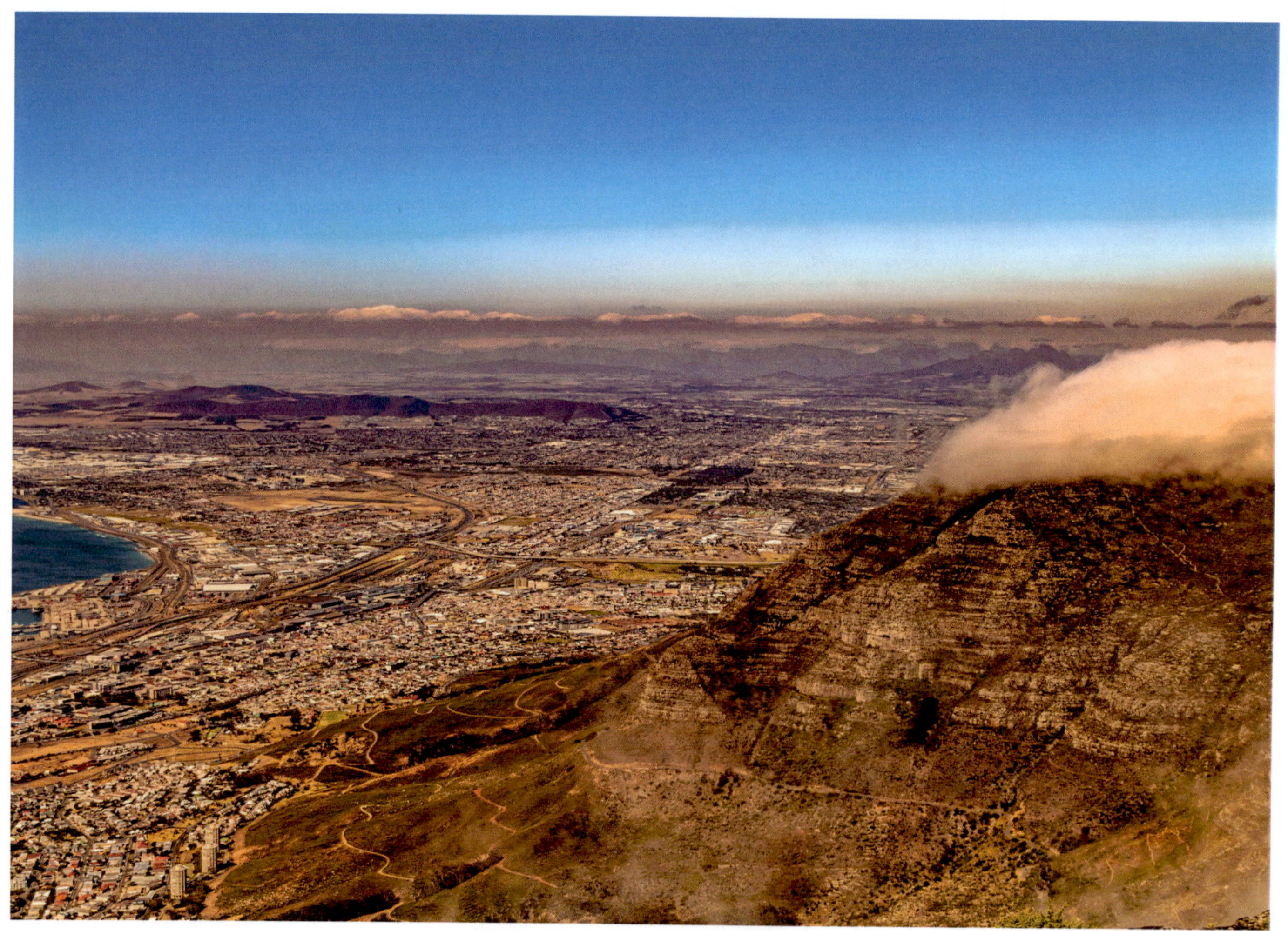

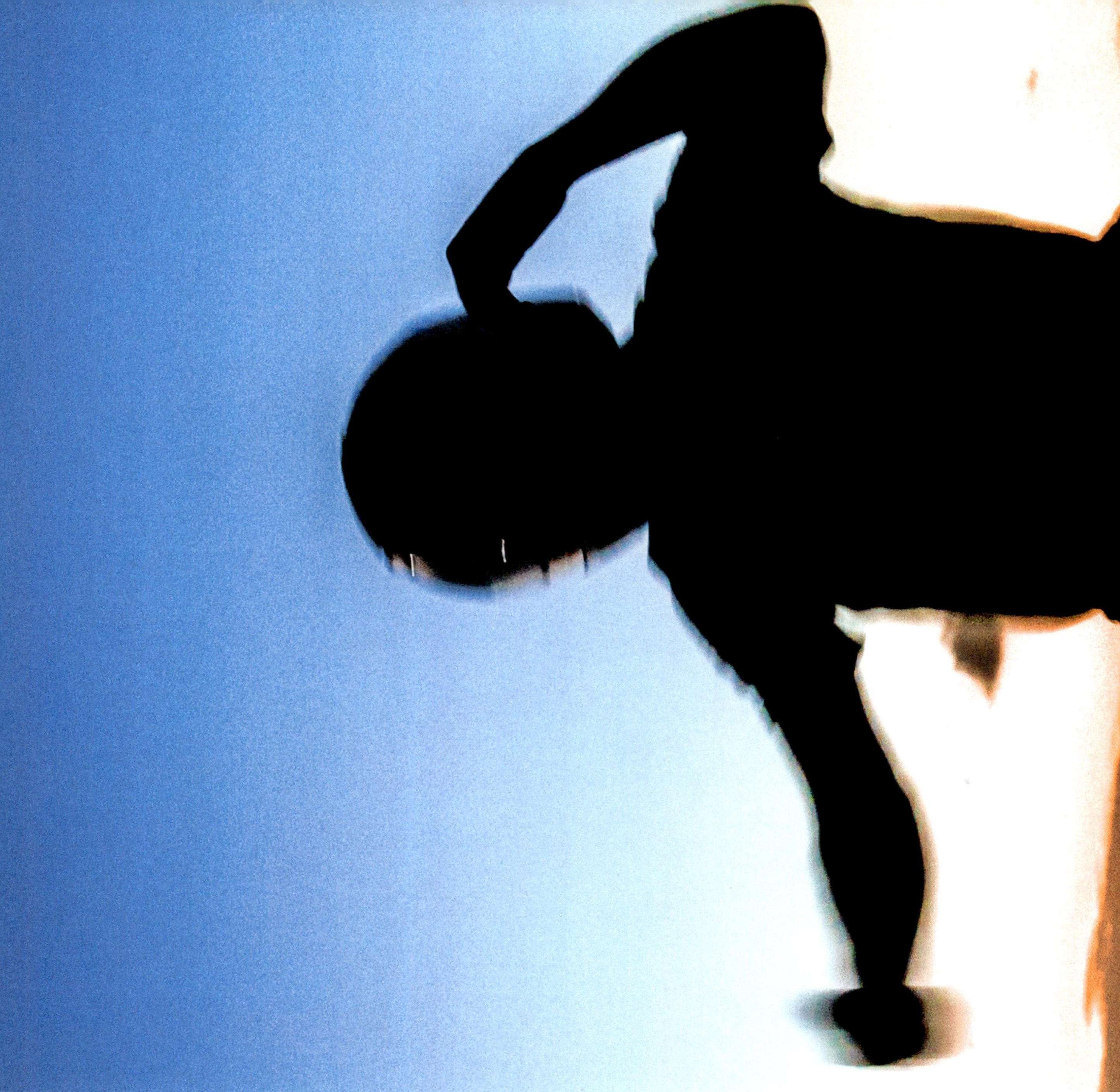
chonkyfire
24mm ÷ f/5 ÷ 1/60
2020

good hands

flash ÷ 29mm ÷ f/11 ÷ 1/100

2016

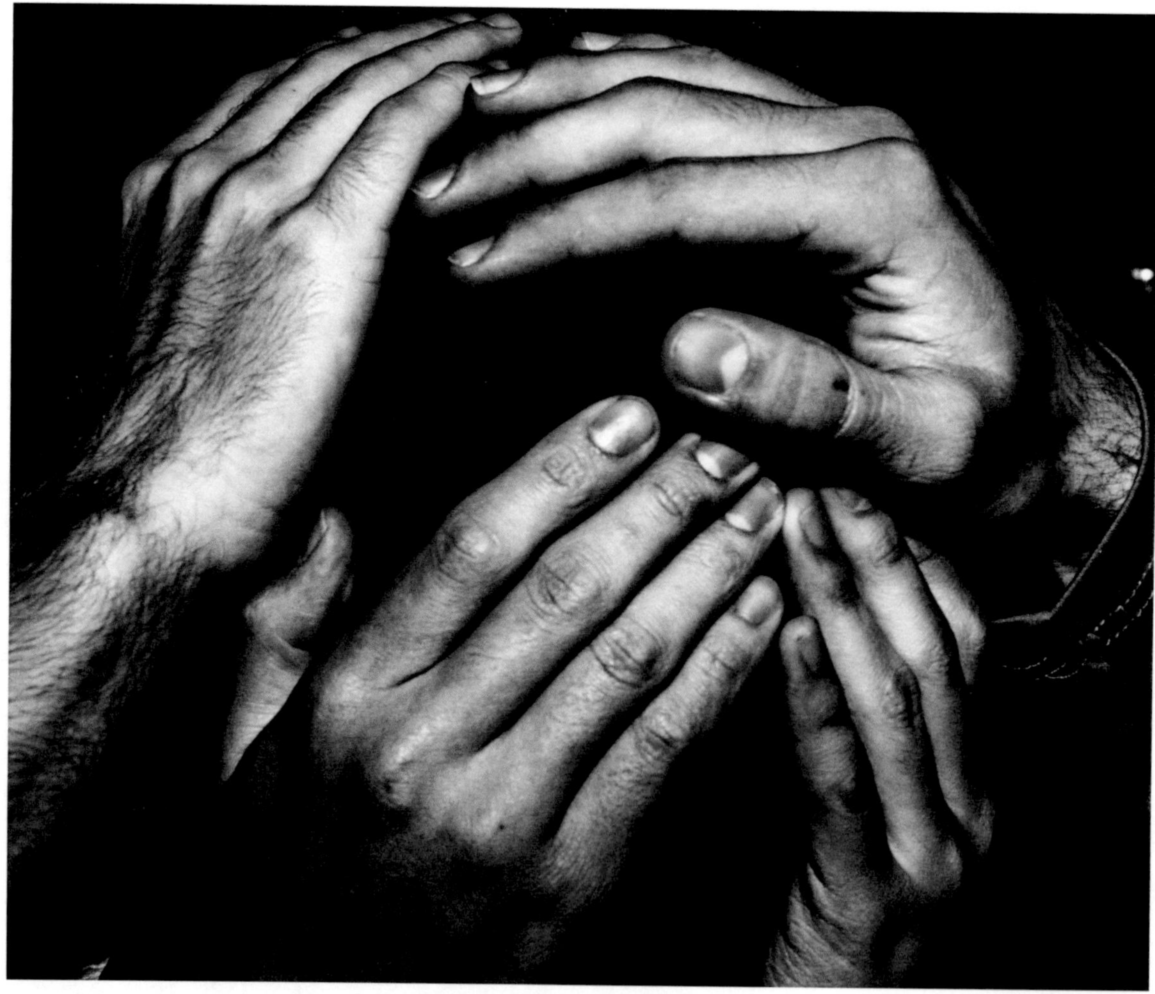

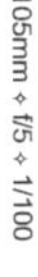

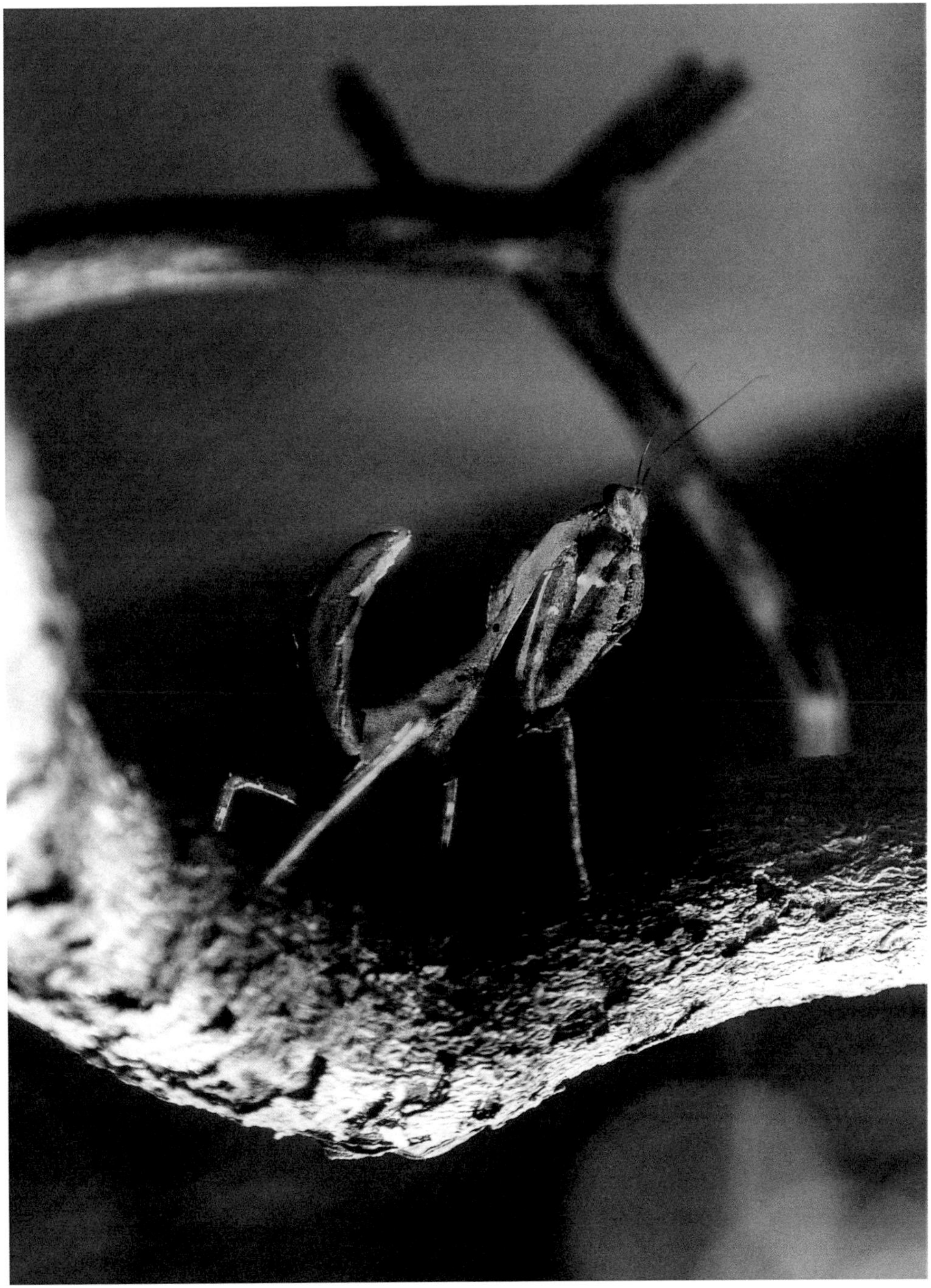

mosque #15
105mm ◇ f/5 ◇ 1/100
2024

2019 untitled 47mm ÷ f/4 ÷ 1/100

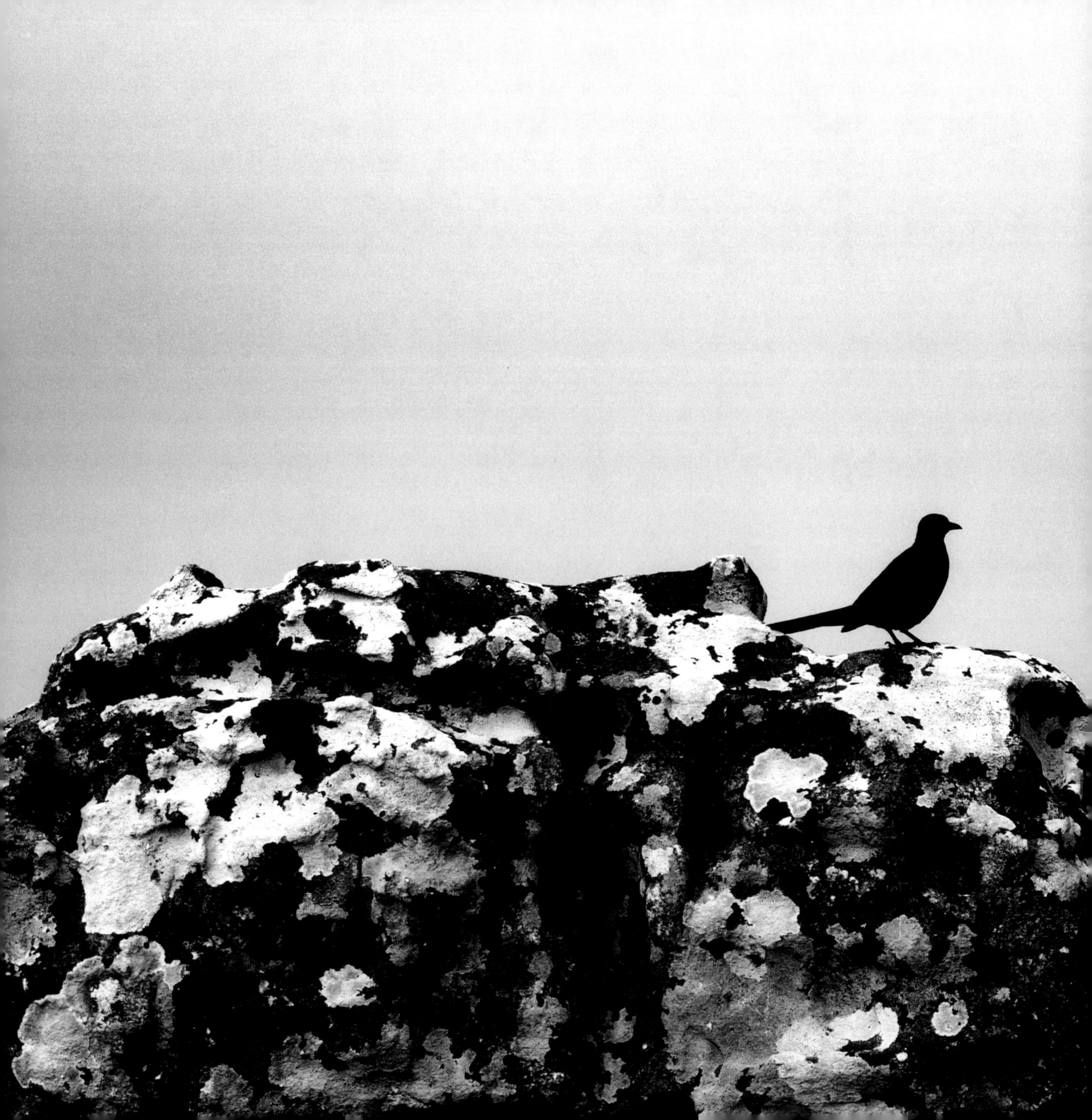

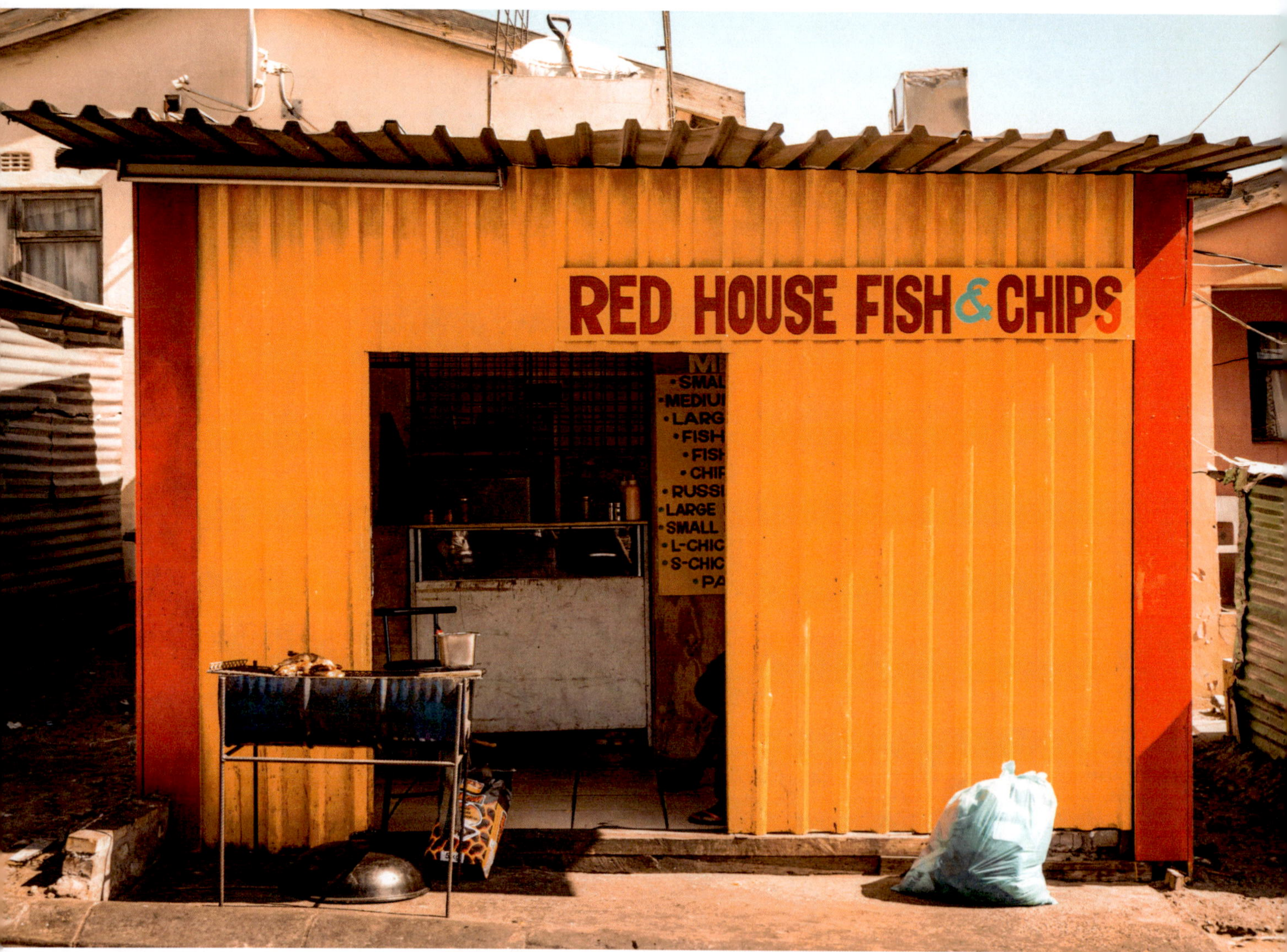

2020

red house fish & chips

24mm ÷ f/11 ÷ 1/200

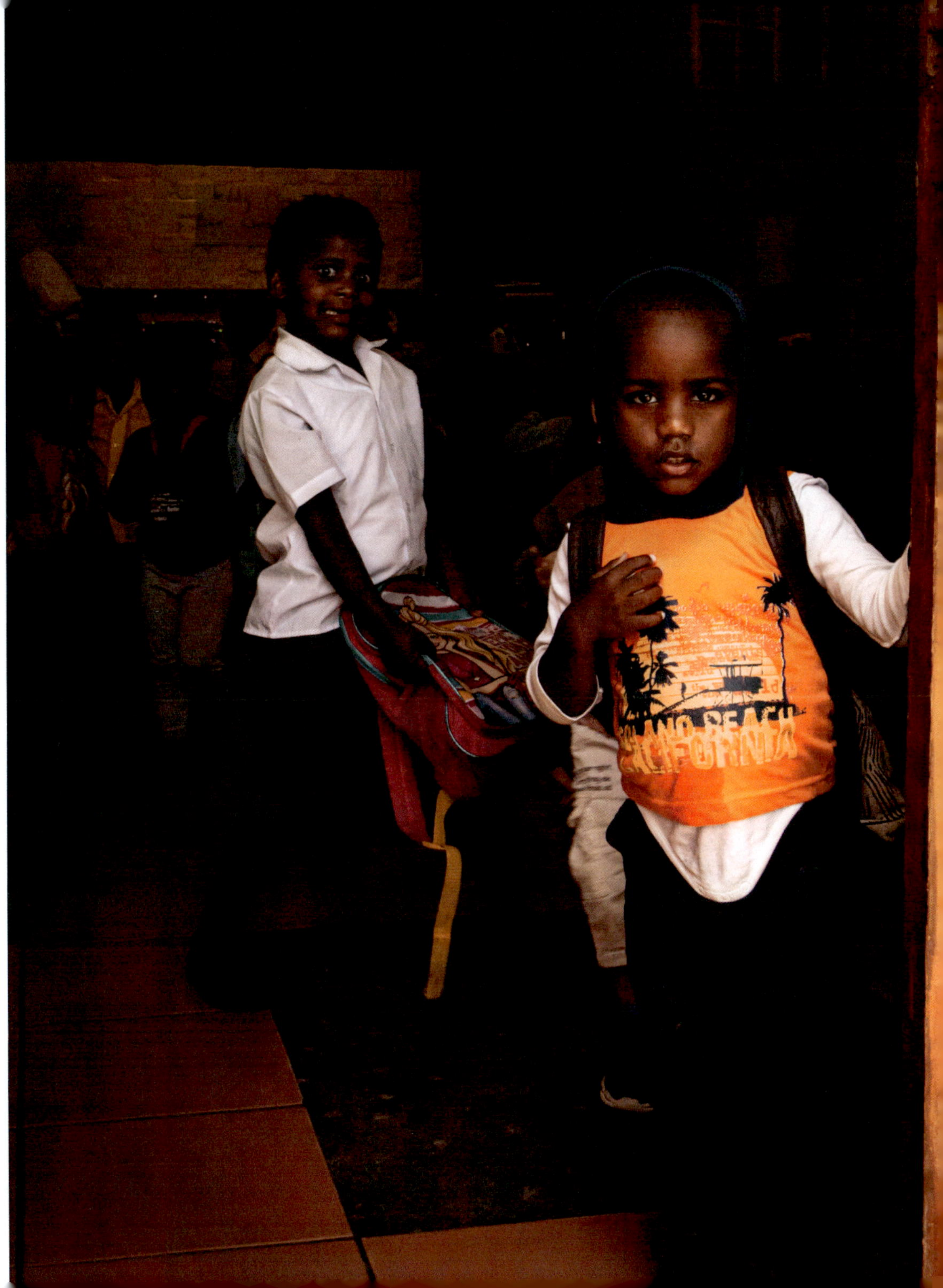

wild berry skittles

24mm ÷ f/11 ÷ 1/100

2020

2021
otis
105mm + f/11 + 1/100
2019

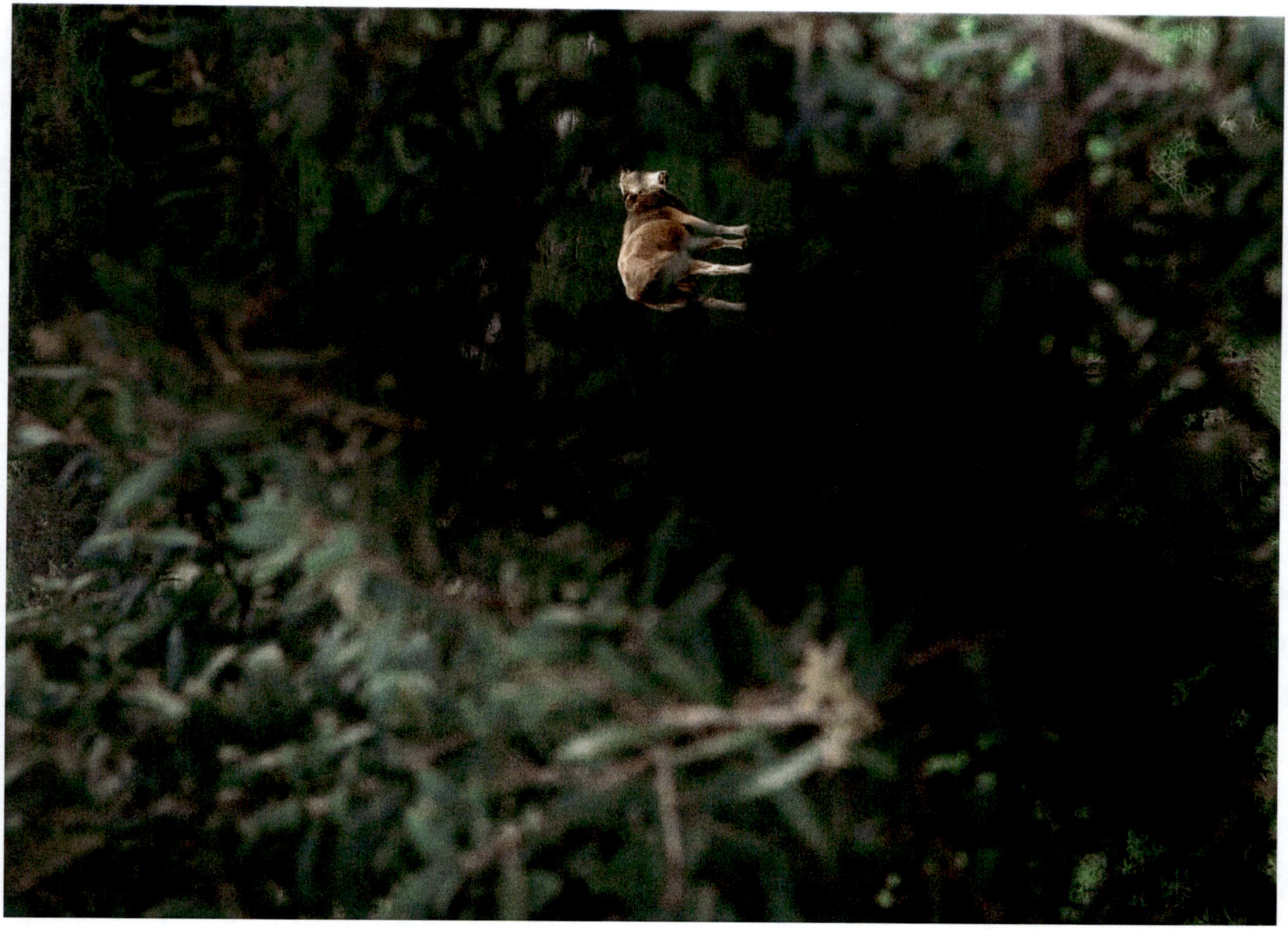

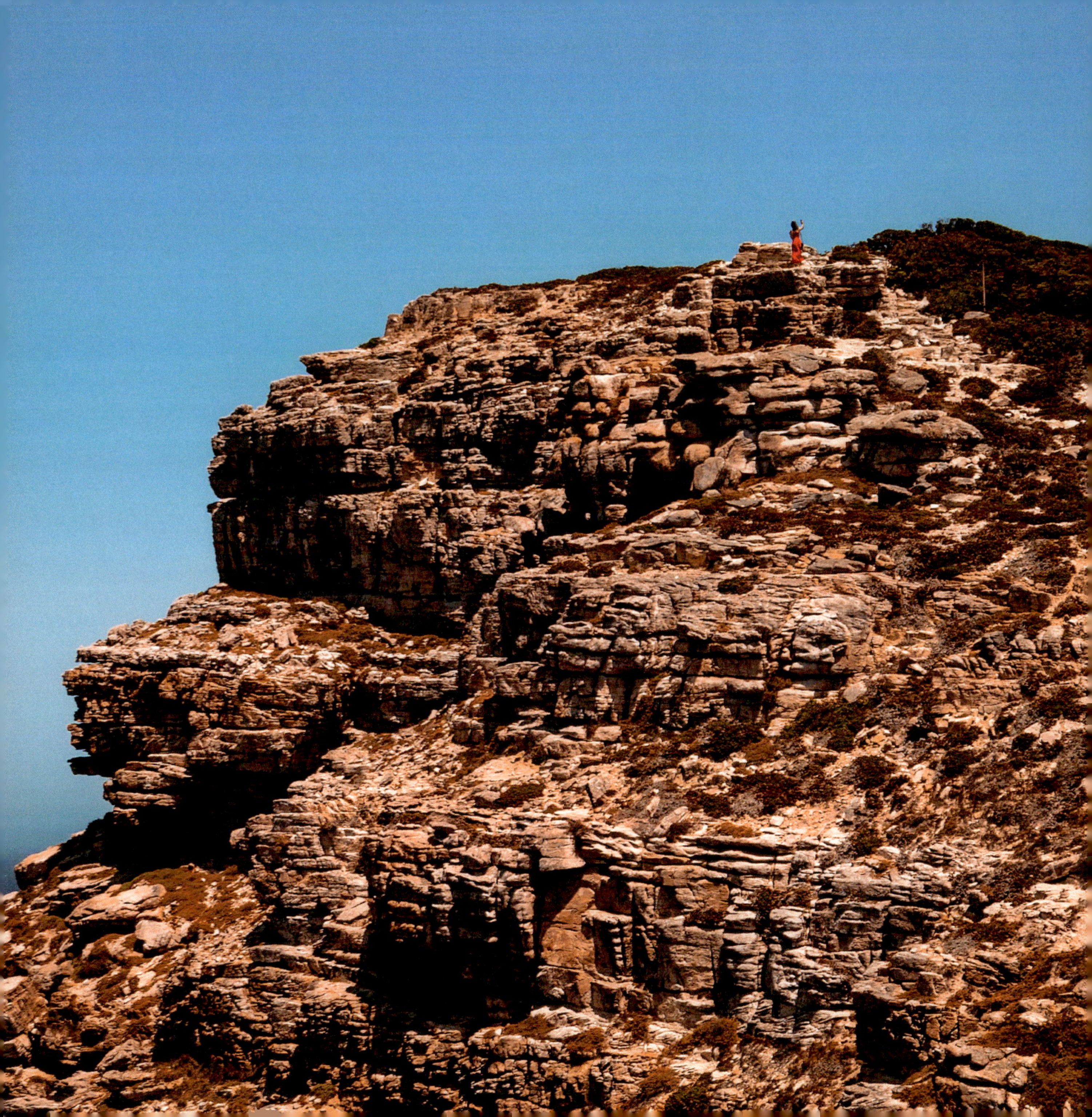

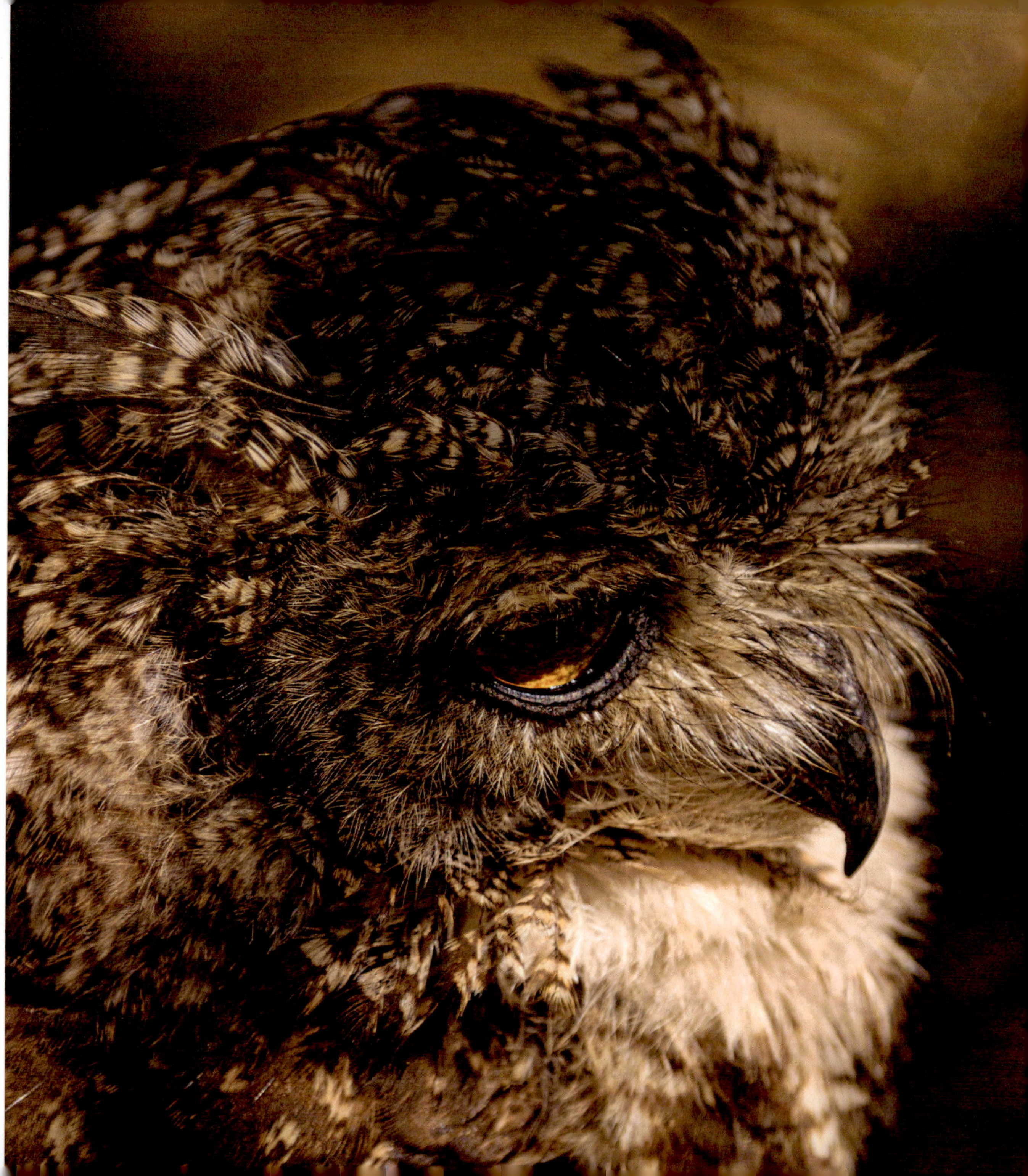

jolson
98mm ÷ f/4 ÷ 1/500
2023

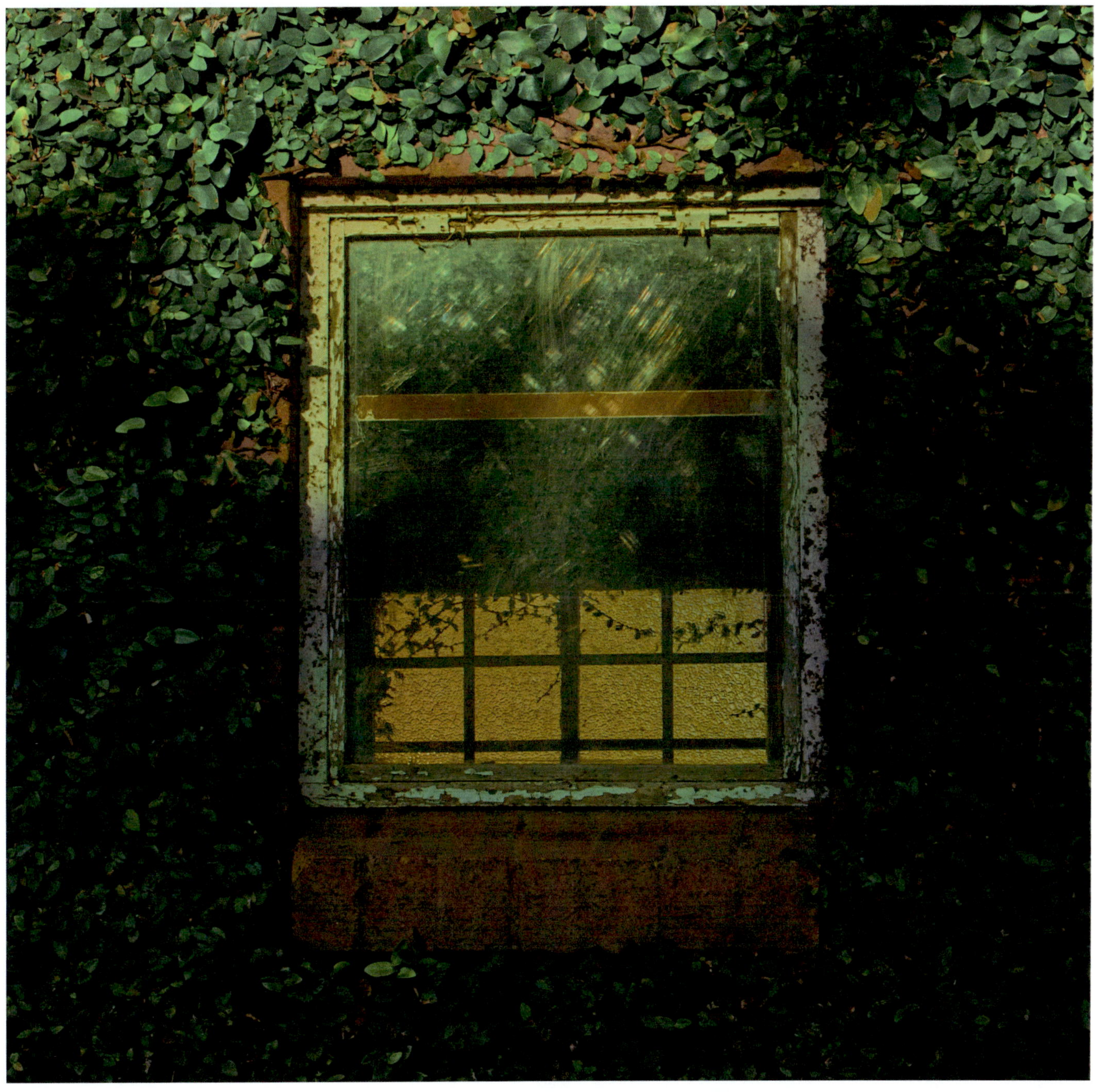

window #33   47mm ÷ f/11 ÷ 1/100   2017

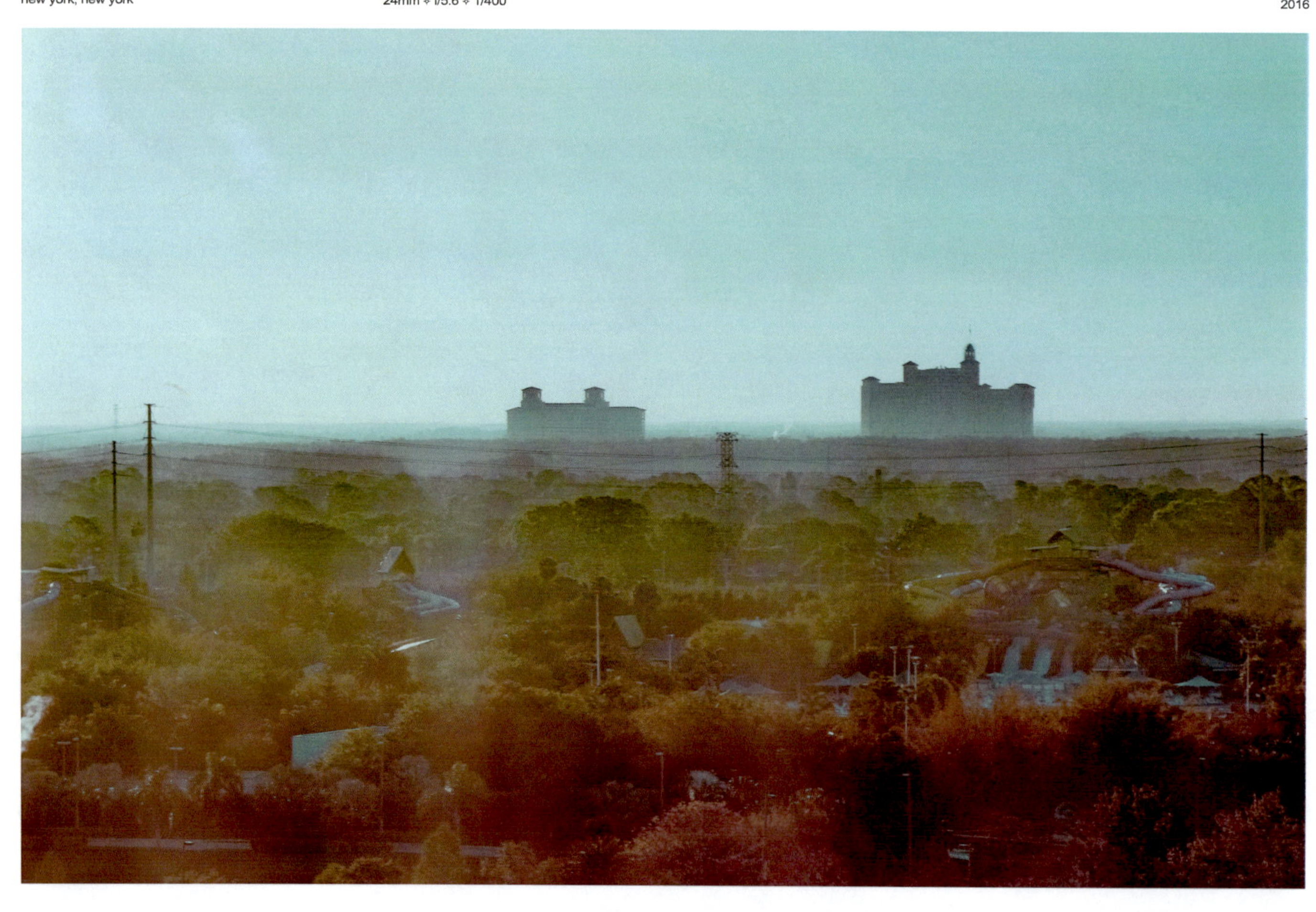

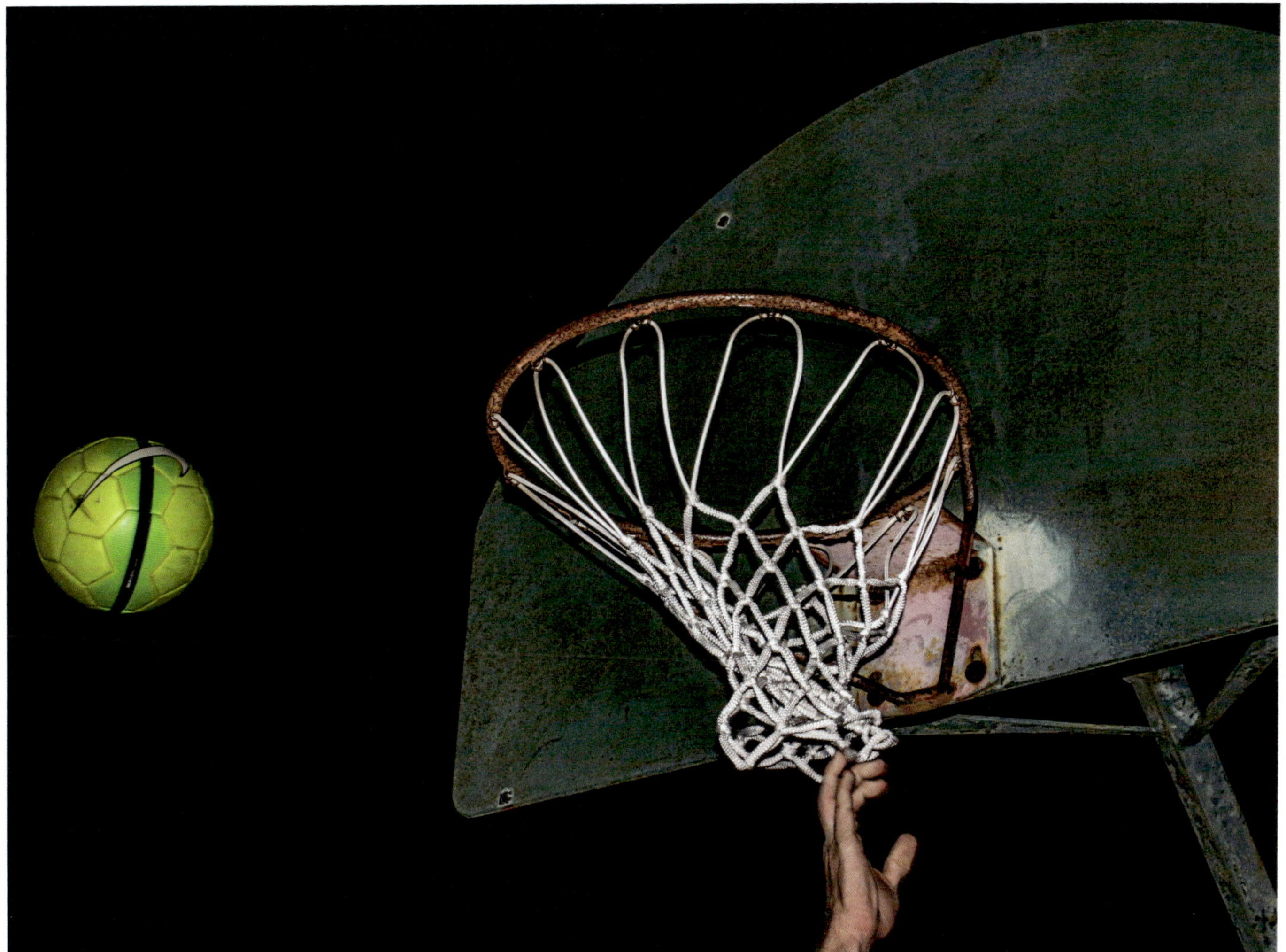

like mike?
36mm ÷ f/11 ÷ 1/160
2017

little light machines & tools:

canon rebel t3

canon ae-1

samsung galaxy s8

lightroom

kodak kb10

canon powershot sd800

markers & saran wrap

www.ingramcontent.com/pod-product-compliance
Lightning Source LLC
Chambersburg PA
CBRC102036110726
48005CB00009BA/1041